List of Spells

	Date	Incanta	Elixir	Talism	Visual			
1								
2								
3								
4								
5								
6								
7								
8								
9								
10								
11								
12								
13								
14								
15								
16								
17								
18								
19								
20								
21								
22								
23								
24								
25								

List of Spells

	Date	Incantation	Elixir	Talisman/Amulet	Visualization			
26								
27								
28								
29								
30								
31								
32								
33								
34								
35								
36								
37								
38								
39								
40								
41								
42								
43								
44								
45								
46								
47								
48								
49								
50								

List of Spells

	Date	Incantation	Elixir	Talisman/Amulet	Visualization			
51								
52								
53								
54								
55								
56								
57								
58								
59								
60								
61								
62								
63								
64								
65								
66								
67								
68								
69								
70								
71								
72								
73								
74								
75								

List of Spells

	Date	Incantation	Elixir	Talisman/Amulet	Visualization			
76								
77								
78								
79								
80								
81								
82								
83								
84								
85								
86								
87								
88								
89								
90								
Wheel of the Year								
Useful Symbols								
Notes								

A Spell For

Inspiration

Malevolent or Benevolent?

You Will Need

How to Cast

Secrets of Success

Use History & Efficacy

2

A Spell For

Malevolent or Benevolent?

Inspiration

You Will Need

How to Cast

Secrets of Success

Use History & Efficacy

A Spell For

Inspiration

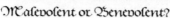
Malevolent or Benevolent?

You Will Need

How to Cast

Secrets of Success

Use History & Efficacy

4

A Spell For

Malevolent or Benevolent?

Inspiration

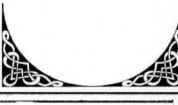

You Will Need

How to Cast

Secrets of Success

Use History & Efficacy

A Spell For

5

Inspiration

Malevolent or Benevolent?

You Will Need

How to Cast

Secrets of Success

Use History & Efficacy

6

A Spell For

Malevolent or Benevolent?

Inspiration

You Will Need

How to Cast

Secrets of Success

Use History & Efficacy

A Spell For

7

Inspiration

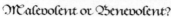
Malevolent or Benevolent?

You Will Need

How to Cast

Secrets of Success

Use History & Efficacy

8

A Spell For

Malevolent or Benevolent?

Inspiration

You Will Need

How to Cast

Secrets of Success

Use History & Efficacy

A Spell For

9

Inspiration

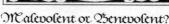
Malevolent or Benevolent?

You Will Need

How to Cast

Secrets of Success

Use History & Efficacy

10

A Spell For

Inspiration

Malevolent or Benevolent?

You Will Need

How to Cast

Secrets of Success

Use History & Efficacy

A Spell For

11

Inspiration

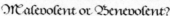
Malevolent or Benevolent?

You Will Need

How to Cast

Secrets of Success

Use History & Efficacy

12

A Spell For

Malevolent or Benevolent?

Inspiration

You Will Need

How to Cast

Secrets of Success

Use History & Efficacy

A Spell For

13

Inspiration

Malevolent or Benevolent?

You Will Need

How to Cast

Secrets of Success

Use History & Efficacy

14

A Spell For

Inspiration

Malevolent or Benevolent?

You Will Need

How to Cast

Secrets of Success

Use History & Efficacy

A Spell For

15

You Will Need

Inspiration

Malevolent or Benevolent?

How to Cast

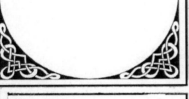

Secrets of Success

Use History & Efficacy

16

Malevolent or Benevolent?

A Spell For

Inspiration

How to Cast

You Will Need

Secrets of Success

Use History & Efficacy

A Spell For

Inspiration

Malevolent or Benevolent?

You Will Need

How to Cast

Secrets of Success

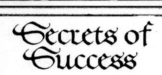

Use History & Efficacy

18

Malevolent or Benevolent?

A Spell For

Inspiration

You Will Need

How to Cast

Secrets of Success

Use History & Efficacy

A Spell For

19

Malevolent or Benevolent?

Inspiration

You Will Need

How to Cast

Secrets of Success

Use History & Efficacy

20

Malevolent or Benevolent?

A Spell For

Inspiration

You Will Need

How to Cast

Secrets of Success

Use History & Efficacy

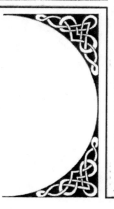

A Spell For

21

Malevolent or Benevolent?

Inspiration

You Will Need

How to Cast

Secrets of Success

Use History & Efficacy

22

A Spell For

Malevolent or Benevolent?

Inspiration

You Will Need

How to Cast

Secrets of Success

Use History & Efficacy

A Spell For

Inspiration

Malevolent or Benevolent?

You Will Need

How to Cast

Secrets of Success

Use History & Efficacy

24

Malevolent or Benevolent?

A Spell For

Inspiration

You Will Need

How to Cast

Secrets of Success

Use History & Efficacy

A Spell For

Inspiration

Malevolent or Benevolent?

You Will Need

How to Cast

Secrets of Success

Use History & Efficacy

26

Malevolent or Benevolent?

A Spell For

Inspiration

How to Cast

You Will Need

Secrets of Success

Use History & Efficacy

A Spell For

27

You Will Need

Inspiration

Malevolent or Benevolent?

How to Cast

Secrets of Success

Use History & Efficacy

28

A Spell For

Inspiration

You Will Need

Malevolent or Benevolent?

How to Cast

Secrets of Success

Use History & Efficacy

A Spell For

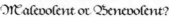
Malevolent or Benevolent?

You Will Need

Inspiration

How to Cast

Secrets of Success

Use History & Efficacy

30

A Spell For

Malevolent or Benevolent?

Inspiration

You Will Need

How to Cast

Secrets of Success

Use History & Efficacy

A Spell For

31

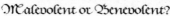
Malevolent or Benevolent?

You Will Need

Inspiration

How to Cast

Secrets of Success

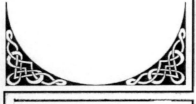

Use History & Efficacy

32

Malevolent or Benevolent?

A Spell For

Inspiration

You Will Need

How to Cast

Secrets of Success

Use History & Efficacy

A Spell For

Inspiration

Malevolent or Benevolent?

You Will Need

How to Cast

Secrets of Success

Use History & Efficacy

34

Malevolent or Benevolent?

A Spell For

Inspiration

How to Cast

You Will Need

Secrets of Success

Use History & Efficacy

A Spell For

35

Inspiration

Malevolent or Benevolent?

You Will Need

How to Cast

Secrets of Success

Use History & Efficacy

36

Malevolent or Benevolent?

A Spell For

Inspiration

You Will Need

How to Cast

Secrets of Success

Use History & Efficacy

A Spell For

37

Malevolent or Benevolent?

Inspiration

You Will Need

How to Cast

Secrets of Success

Use History & Efficacy

38

A Spell For

Inspiration

Malevolent or Benevolent?

You Will Need

How to Cast

Secrets of Success

Use History & Efficacy

A Spell For

39

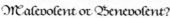
Malevolent or Benevolent?

Inspiration

You Will Need

How to Cast

Secrets of Success

Use History & Efficacy

40

Malevolent or Benevolent?

A Spell For

Inspiration

How to Cast

You Will Need

Secrets of Success

Use History & Efficacy

A Spell For

41

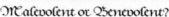

Malevolent or Benevolent?

Inspiration

You Will Need

How to Cast

Secrets of Success

Use History & Efficacy

42

A Spell For

Malevolent or Benevolent?

Inspiration

You Will Need

How to Cast

Secrets of Success

Use History & Efficacy

A Spell For

43

Inspiration

You Will Need

Malevolent or Benevolent?

How to Cast

Secrets of Success

Use History & Efficacy

44

A Spell For

Malevolent or Benevolent?

Inspiration

You Will Need

How to Cast

Secrets of Success

Use History & Efficacy

A Spell For

Inspiration

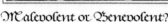
Malevolent or Benevolent?

You Will Need

How to Cast

Secrets of Success

Use History & Efficacy

46

Malevolent or Benevolent?

A Spell For

Inspiration

You Will Need

How to Cast

Secrets of Success

Use History & Efficacy

A Spell For

Inspiration

Malevolent or Benevolent?

You Will Need

How to Cast

Secrets of Success

Use History & Efficacy

48

A Spell For

Inspiration

Malevolent or Benevolent?

You Will Need

How to Cast

Secrets of Success

Use History & Efficacy

A Spell For

Inspiration

You Will Need

Malevolent or Benevolent?

How to Cast

Secrets of Success

Use History & Efficacy

50

Malevolent or Benevolent?

A Spell For

Inspiration

How to Cast

You Will Need

Secrets of Success

Use History & Efficacy

A Spell For

51

Inspiration

Malevolent or Benevolent?

You Will Need

How to Cast

Secrets of Success

Use History & Efficacy

52

Malevolent or Benevolent?

A Spell For

Inspiration

How to Cast

You Will Need

Secrets of Success

Use History & Efficacy

A Spell For

Inspiration

Malevolent or Benevolent?

You Will Need

How to Cast

Secrets of Success

Use History & Efficacy

54

Malevolent or Benevolent?

A Spell For

Inspiration

You Will Need

How to Cast

Secrets of Success

Use History & Efficacy

A Spell For

55

Inspiration

Malevolent or Benevolent?

You Will Need

How to Cast

Secrets of Success

Use History & Efficacy

56

Malevolent or Benevolent?

A Spell For

Inspiration

You Will Need

How to Cast

Secrets of Success

Use History & Efficacy

A Spell For

Inspiration

Malevolent or Benevolent?

You Will Need

How to Cast

Secrets of Success

Use History & Efficacy

58

A Spell For

Inspiration

Malevolent or Benevolent?

You Will Need

How to Cast

Secrets of Success

Use History
& Efficacy

A Spell For

Inspiration

Malevolent or Benevolent?

You Will Need

How to Cast

Secrets of Success

Use History & Efficacy

60

A Spell For

Inspiration

Malevolent or Benevolent?

You Will Need

How to Cast

Secrets of Success

Use History & Efficacy

A Spell For

Inspiration

Malevolent or Benevolent?

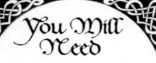

You Will Need

How to Cast

Secrets of Success

Use History & Efficacy

62

A Spell for

Malevolent or Benevolent?

Inspiration

You Will Need

How to Cast

Secrets of Success

Use History & Efficacy

A Spell For

63

Malevolent or Benevolent?

You Will Need

Inspiration

How to Cast

Secrets of Success

Use History & Efficacy

64

A Spell For

Inspiration

Malevolent or Benevolent?

You Will Need

How to Cast

Secrets of Success

Use History & Efficacy

A Spell For

65

You Will Need

Inspiration

Malevolent or Benevolent?

How to Cast

Secrets of Success

Use History & Efficacy

66

A Spell For

Inspiration

Malevolent or Benevolent?

How to Cast

You Will Need

Secrets of Success

Use History & Efficacy

A Spell For

67

You Will Need

Inspiration

How to Cast

Secrets of Success

Use History & Efficacy

68

Malevolent or Benevolent?

A Spell For

Inspiration

How to Cast

You Will Need

Secrets of Success

Use History & Efficacy

A Spell For

Inspiration

You Will Need

Malevolent or Benevolent?

How to Cast

Secrets of Success

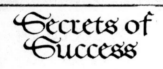

Use History & Efficacy

70

A Spell For

Malevolent or Benevolent?

Inspiration

You Will Need

How to Cast

Secrets of Success

Use History & Efficacy

A Spell For

Inspiration

You Will Need

How to Cast

Secrets of Success

Use History & Efficacy

72

A Spell For

Inspiration

Malevolent or Benevolent?

You Will Need

How to Cast

Secrets of Success

Use History & Efficacy

A Spell For

73

Malevolent or Benevolent?

You Will Need

Inspiration

How to Cast

Secrets of Success

Use History & Efficacy

74

A Spell For

Inspiration

Malevolent or Benevolent?

You Will Need

How to Cast

Secrets of Success

Use History & Efficacy

A Spell For

75

You Will Need

Inspiration

Malevolent or Benevolent?

How to Cast

Secrets of Success

Use History & Efficacy

76

A Spell For

Inspiration

Malevolent or Benevolent?

How to Cast

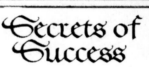

You Will Need

Secrets of Success

Use History & Efficacy

A Spell For

Inspiration

Malevolent or Benevolent?

You Will Need

How to Cast

Secrets of Success

Use History & Efficacy

78

A Spell For

Inspiration

Malevolent or Benevolent?

How to Cast

You Will Need

Secrets of Success

Use History & Efficacy

A Spell For

Malevolent or Benevolent?

You Will Need

Inspiration

How to Cast

Secrets of Success

Use History & Efficacy

80

A Spell For

Inspiration

Malevolent or Benevolent?

You Will Need

How to Cast

Secrets of Success

Use History & Efficacy

A Spell For

81

Malevolent or Benevolent?

Inspiration

You Will Need

How to Cast

Secrets of Success

Use History & Efficacy

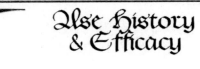

82

Malevolent or Benevolent?

A Spell For

Inspiration

How to Cast

You Will Need

Secrets of Success

Use History & Efficacy

A Spell For

Malevolent or Benevolent?

Inspiration

You Will Need

How to Cast

Secrets of Success

Use History & Efficacy

84

A Spell For

Inspiration

Malevolent or Benevolent?

You Will Need

How to Cast

Secrets of Success

Use History & Efficacy

A Spell For

85

You Will Need

Inspiration

Malevolent or Benevolent?

How to Cast

Secrets of Success

Use History & Efficacy

86

A Spell For

Malevolent or Benevolent?

Inspiration

You Will Need

How to Cast

Secrets of Success

Use History & Efficacy

A Spell For

Malevolent or Benevolent?

Inspiration

You Will Need

How to Cast

Secrets of Success

Use History & Efficacy

88

A Spell For

Inspiration

Malevolent or Benevolent?

You Will Need

How to Cast

Secrets of Success

Use History & Efficacy

A Spell For

89

Malevolent or Benevolent?

Inspiration

You Will Need

How to Cast

Secrets of Success

Use History & Efficacy

90

A Spell For

Inspiration

Malevolent or Benevolent?

You Will Need

How to Cast

Secrets of Success

Use History & Efficacy

Notes

Thanks for choosing our Spell Book. If you'd be willing to consider posting an Amazon review with a photo we'd be *most* grateful because many customers really struggle with loading the Look Inside facility.

We also publish affordable: Reading Logs, Blank Recipe Books, Daily Planners, Meal Planners & much more. To take a look, or get in touch, visit smartbookx.com.

Manufactured by Amazon.ca
Acheson, AB

12825274R00055